Antoine
Lavoisier
Founder of Modern Chemistry

Lynn Van Gorp, M.S.

Physical Science Readers:
Antoine Lavoisier: Founder of Modern Chemistry

Publishing Credits

Editorial Director
Dona Herweck Rice

Creative Director
Lee Aucoin

Associate Editor
Joshua BishopRoby

Illustration Manager
Timothy J. Bradley

Editor-in-Chief
Sharon Coan, M.S.Ed.

Publisher
Rachelle Cracchiolo, M.S.Ed

Science Contributor
Sally Ride Science

Science Consultants
Michael E. Kopecky,
   Science Department Chair,
   Chino Hills High School
Jane Weir, MPhys

Teacher Created Materials
5301 Oceanus Drive
Huntington Beach, CA 92649-1030
http://www.tcmpub.com
ISBN 978-0-7439-0582-4
© 2007 Teacher Created Materials

Table of Contents

Antoine Laurent Lavoisier
(ahn-TWAN loh-RAHN la-vwah-ZYAY) is considered the "Founder of Modern Chemistry." Many scientists are remembered for their research. Lavoisier is not. He is most remembered for the way he changed how scientists study science.

Lavoisier lived in France in the 1700s. People then believed in **alchemy** (AL-kuh-mee). It was an early type of science. Alchemists did not use the **scientific method**. The scientific method is a careful, step-by-step process for proving or disproving something. Alchemists, on the other hand, looked at things such as star patterns and old ideas from ancient philosophers. The alchemists thought they could make gold from other metals like lead. This wasn't true. Many people believed them, anyway.

Antoine Laurent Lavoisier

The cover page of Lavoisier's book

Magic
Many alchemists were thought to be sorcerers or wizards.

Chemistry

Chemistry is the science that deals with the structure, composition, and properties of substances. All substances in the universe are made of **matter**. The building blocks of matter are **atoms**. Atoms combine to make **molecules**. When a substance is made of all the same kind of atoms, it is called an **element**. Matter, all of its parts, how it behaves, and how it is made are all part of chemistry. They are the basic things studied and researched by a chemist.

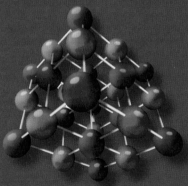

A model of a molecule

In the Beginning

Paris in the 1740s was alive with music, art, and culture. New ideas were happening in science and math. The world was an exciting place. That is, it was alive and exciting for the upper classes. Conditions for the poor were very bad.

For the poor, there were high taxes, filthy living conditions, and terrible health care. Many people who were not among the upper classes were unhappy.

Antoine Laurent Lavoisier was born in Paris, France, on August 26, 1743. His family was very wealthy. His father was a well-known lawyer. His mother was the daughter of a judge in the French Parliament. The parliament is a group of leaders who make laws for a country. The family lived a rich and happy life.

Sadly, Lavoisier's mother died when he was very young. His aunt looked after him and his sister. She dedicated her life to them.

Poor French washerwomen

The Court of Versailles enjoying an outing

Lavoisier's aunt wanted him to have a good education. She did all she could to make that happen. When he was 11 years old, he was sent to one of the best schools in France. He was a hard worker. He received many awards for being a good student.

In 1764, he became a lawyer. He seemed to be following his father's footsteps. His success as a lawyer was growing. The problem was that he loved science. He loved science more than the law.

He decided to dedicate his life to science instead. First, he studied earth science, called geology (jee-OL-uh-jee). Then, he wrote and published a paper on how to improve the lighting in Paris. His early science work got him elected to the Royal Academy of Science in 1768. This was an honor for so young a person.

Lavoisier wanted to spend all of his time working as a scientist. However, he needed money to pay for his equipment and supplies. He worked as a tax collector during the day. This money made it possible for him to work at night on his research.

Scientific instruments of the time showing Lavoisier's oxygen experiment.

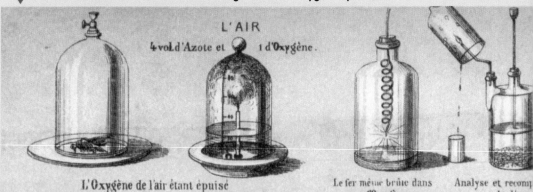

Marie Curie
(1867–1934)

Marie Curie knew the importance of education, too. She was born in Poland in 1867. She shared her love of physics with her father. He worked as a high school physics teacher. In 1891, she went to Paris. She studied at a famous French university. Two years later, she finished at the top of her class.

She became a famous chemist in the field of radiology. She and her husband received the Nobel Prize in 1903. Marie Curie was the first woman to win that award. In 1911, she received a second Nobel Prize.

▲ Lavoisier working on an experiment to find the elements of water

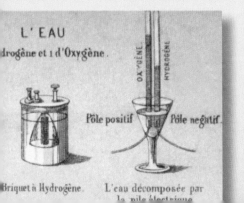

L'EAU
drogène et 1 d'Oxygène.

OXYGÈNE   HYDROGÈNE

Pôle positif   Pôle négatif.

Briquet à Hydrogène.   L'eau décomposée par
                        la pile électrique

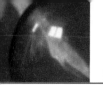

This is Lavoisier with his wife Marie-Anne. An air pump is shown on the table.

Lavoisier married Marie-Anne Pierrette Paulze (muh-REE-AN pee-uh-RET pawl-ZEY). She was the daughter of another member of the tax collection company where he worked. She was just 13 when they married in 1771. It was common for women to marry young then. She began to work with Lavoisier. She helped him with his experiments. She drew detailed pictures and recorded the results. She prepared them to be published. She also learned to read English, which Lavoisier could not do. This helped him to study the work of English scientists.

In 1775, Lavoisier began working for the National Gunpowder Commission. This allowed him to create an excellent lab for his experiments. His lab and his home also became important places for scientists to gather.

Pierre Curie
(1867-1906)

Pierre Curie was a chemist born in Paris. He was married to Marie Curie. The two worked together just as the Lavoisiers had before them.

The Curies studied radioactive (ray-dee-oh-AK-tiv) materials. Pierre experimented with radium (RAY-dee-uhm) on himself. He also kept a sample of it in his pocket. He had no idea that the radium was so harmful. He became frail and was in constant pain. Sadly, he was killed in a road accident in 1906. His wife continued their work on her own.

The Curies' work was so dangerous that the notebooks they used are still radioactive. Before scientists can look at them, they must sign a paper saying they know the notebooks are harmful.

Pierre and Marie Curie

Lavoisier invented this solar furnace to focus the sun's rays to heat his experiments.

Lavoisier was famous for his hard work in the lab. He was very careful with his experiments. He took accurate measurements. Lavoisier protected his findings until he was finished with each project. Once finished, he was happy to share them.

Lavoisier also studied other scientists' work. At the time, some people thought he was stealing. When he started with what other scientists learned, though, Lavoisier was able to learn new things. Reading other scientists' work became a new standard for scientists. Today it is an important part of science.

Lavoisier also shared his political views with those who came to his home and lab. Many **freethinkers** were drawn there. In France, there was a growing unease. People did not feel the same support for the government that they had in the past. Many people were very poor and unhappy. They thought the country's leaders were unfair. People who came to Lavoisier's home and lab talked about science and politics. Lavoisier believed that France needed to be reformed. He joined a committee that was organized to make a difference. The committee proposed new taxes. It suggested changes for hospitals and prisons.

Lavoisier and his friends on the committee tried to change conditions in France to make life easier. Not many things changed, though. The country was headed for revolution.

Linus Pauling
(1901–1994)

One of the most important chemists of modern times was Linus Pauling (LIE-nuhs PAW-ling). In 1954, he was awarded the Nobel Prize in chemistry. His work described the nature of the **chemical bond**. That is the force that holds atoms together in molecules. In 1962, Pauling was awarded the Nobel Peace Prize. He worked to keep dangerous nuclear tests safe underground.

Here is a fun fact about Linus Pauling. His good friend was the cartoonist Charles Schulz. Schulz is famous for his *Peanuts* comic strip. He named Charlie Brown's friend Linus after his own friend, Linus Pauling.

Important Work

During his life as a scientist, Lavoisier did some important new work. The work and how he did it changed chemistry forever.

Law of Conservation of Mass

In chemistry, a **chemical reaction** happens when one or more elements react and turn into a new substance (the product). Remember that elements are made of the same atom. They are pure. To be a reaction, the elements must act together and a chemical change must happen. For example, oxygen and iron are elements. When they come together, there is a reaction. They become rust.

Lavoisier measured the **mass** of each substance before it reacted. Mass is the amount of matter a substance has. Then, he measured the mass of new substances after the reaction. He proved that matter is never lost or gained. Even when something new is made, mass stays the same. He called this law **Conservation** (kon-ser-VAY-shuhn) **of Mass.** To be conserved is to remain the same. Matter can change its state, but its mass stays the same.

Night Owl
Lavoisier did most of his research at night. During the day, he worked at his other jobs.

Dorothy Crowfoot Hodgkin (1910–1994)

In 1964, Dorothy Hodgkin won the Nobel Prize in chemistry. She used X-ray **crystallography** (kris-tuhl-OG-ruh-fee) to see the shape of certain substances. Crystallography is a branch of science that deals with how crystals are made and how they behave. A crystal is a special kind of mineral. Its molecules all line up in a regular pattern. This gives the crystal a sharply defined shape.

⬆ Lavoisier proved that metal weighs more when it rusts. He also identified the element oxygen that combines with iron to create rust. The added oxygen makes the iron weigh more.

Existence of Oxygen

There are 93 different elements that occur in nature. Many elements were not known until recent times. Oxygen is one important element. It is in the air we breathe. Water is made partly of oxygen, too.

Lavoisier was the first to identify and name oxygen as an element. He named 33 other substances as elements, too! He defined an element as a substance that could not break down into a simpler substance. That definition remains today.

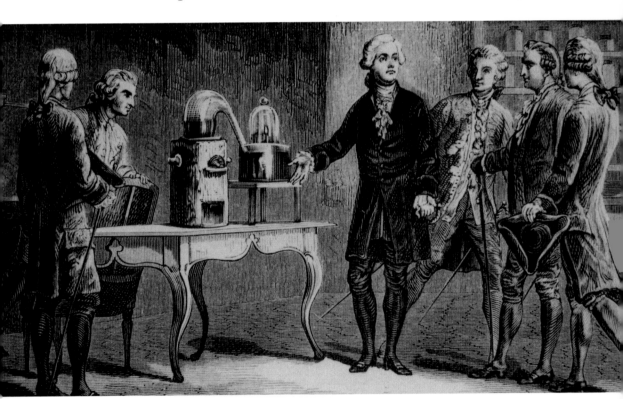

⬆ Lavoisier is shown here conducting his experiment showing that air was composed mainly of oxygen and nitrogen. He identified oxygen as a gas that burns well. He also identified nitrogen as a gas that doesn't burn well.

Rosalind Franklin
(1920–1958)

Rosalind Franklin was an important chemist of modern times. She created the first usable X-ray pictures of DNA. DNA is part of every living thing. It determines who and what a living thing will be, how it will look, and more. Your DNA is the reason for such things as why your eyes are the color they are and why you are the height you are.

To take her pictures, Franklin used **X-ray diffraction** (duh-FRAK-shuhn). X-rays can take pictures of very tiny structures. With diffraction, the X-rays bounce off the molecule and leave a pattern.

Rosalind Franklin worked hard, but her work was not well known. Many thought it was because of prejudice against her as a woman. There is some reason to believe that others may have taken her work and used it as their own after her early death.

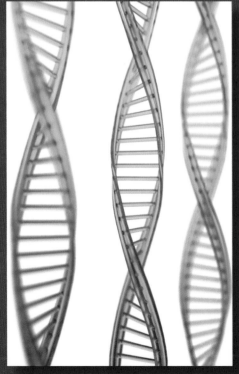

DNA strands

Naming Compounds

Two or more elements can combine to form a substance. That substance is called a **compound**. Lavoisier wanted everyone to label compounds the same way. Organization in science is very important. In that way, each scientist can use the work of other scientists. Lavoisier created a system in which the name of a compound was linked to the elements in it.

These are the rules for naming simple compounds with two different elements:

- The first word is the name of the first element.
- The second word tells you the second element and how many atoms there are of it in the compound.
- The second word ends in –*ide*.

For example, carbon and oxygen make a compound. It is called carbon dioxide (dahy-OK-sahyd). *Carbon* is the name of the first element. *Di* means two, or two atoms. *Ox* stands for oxygen. *Ide* is the chosen ending. Put them together and you have *carbon dioxide*.

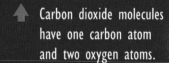

Carbon dioxide molecules have one carbon atom and two oxygen atoms.

Dmitri Mendeléev (1834–1907)

Dmitri Mendeléev (duh-ME-tree MEN-duh-LAY-yef) also knew that organization is important in science. He was the first scientist to organize the elements into groups. He created the **Periodic Table**. It is still used by scientists when working with the elements.

ПЕРИОДИЧЕСКАЯ СИСТЕМА ЭЛЕМЕНТОВ

Mendeléev's Table of Elements

Trying to Make a Difference

Lavoisier used his research findings to help people. He believed that scientists have a duty to improve the world around them. For example, he showed farmers how to grow better crops and raise stronger cattle. He gave farmers money to buy grain during the famine of 1788.

While working on his science, Lavoisier continued his interest in government. He wrote a report on France's finances. He wanted to make things better for France. He thought the government was failing the people, especially the poor.

During that time, France was ruled by a king and queen. They were King Louis (LOO-ee) XVI and Queen Marie-Antoinette (muh-REE an-twuh-NET). At first, they were well loved by the people. However, France's troubles grew. The poor were very unhappy. They were taxed more and more but had less and less. The rich seemed to grow richer and richer.

This picture shows the court of King Louis XVI and Marie-Antoinette with visitor Benjamin Franklin.

Mario Molina
(1943–)

Dr. Mario Molina wanted to help people. He was born and raised in Mexico City. His city had the worst air pollution in the world. Molina knew he could use chemistry to improve the air.

He knew something was damaging the earth's ozone layer. The ozone layer is important. It filters out most of the sun's harmful rays. It protects life on Earth. He believed that chlorofluorocarbons (**CFCs**) were causing ozone problems. CFCs are chemicals used in aerosol cans, plastic foam, and other things. Many scientists did not believe him. After much hard work, he found evidence to support his theory. He has influenced many governments to cut their use of CFCs.

In 1995, Mario Molina was the first person to receive a Nobel Prize for research into man-made problems. He also received an honorary Doctor of Science degree from Tufts University.

The hole in the ozone layer

People blamed the king and queen for their poverty. They believed the king and queen did not want to help them. The people grew so angry that they revolted. Now, the rulers were in great danger. In 1789, the French Revolution began.

The king and queen were overthrown. Following the war, thousands of executions took place. Many used the guillotine (GEE-uh-teen). The guillotine is a device that chops off a person's head by dropping down a sharp blade. King Louis XVI was sent to the guillotine in early 1793. Queen Marie-Antoinette was also killed in this way later that year.

Guillotine
The guillotine remained a legal way to execute criminals in France until 1981.

Lavoisier had worked for King Louis XVI. He had been a tax collector. Soon after the revolution began, some news writers began to say bad things about Lavoisier. They accused him of crimes against the people because he was a tax collector.

The truth was that Lavoisier was an important figure in bringing about the revolution. He had worked to bring about change. He wanted to make things better for everyone. The new leaders did not care. All the members of the tax collecting group were arrested on May 8, 1794.

Painting of a battle from the French Revolution

Death by Guillotine

🔺 Crowds of peasants would gather to watch the executions of wealthy people.

Lavoisier did not realize that his own life was in danger. He had a chance to flee France, but he did not. He wanted to stay and continue his research. He was arrested with all the others.

All the tax collectors were put to trial on the day of the arrest. The trial lasted less than a day. They were found guilty and sentenced to die. On May 8, Lavoisier was sent to the guillotine with all the others. He asked for more time to complete his scientific work. The judge said, "The Republic has no need of scientists." Much of Lavoisier's work was left unfinished.

His wife was not allowed to give him a proper burial. His body was thrown into a common grave. Common graves were used to bury those who could not afford graves and those who were unknown at death.

After Lavoisier's death, his wife ran a science salon. It gave scientists a place to do their research. They continued Lavoisier's work in his place.

That is the way of science. One scientist's work inspires another. Scientists for years to come will thank Lavoisier for the legacy he left behind. Just like Lavoisier, they use the work he and others did to continue to learn new things.

Modern scientists can thank Lavoisier for his legacy.

Chemist: Marye Anne Fox

University of California, San Diego

Cooking Up a Storm

Chemistry is like cooking. A chemist can mix different ingredients to create something new. Maybe it is a new medicine or a new type of plastic.

Some chemists, such as Marye Anne Fox, can even create new ingredients. "It's fascinating because you can make new things that didn't exist before," she says. Fox's new chemicals

Marye Anne Fox in her lab

Being There

"The ability to work in teams is increasingly important in chemistry," Fox says. Do you like to work together with other people?

CH_2Cl_2

are being used to improve the world. They may be used to make better solar-powered cars. They also make skyscraper windows that do not need cleaning.

Fox does not spend all her time in the lab. She has written for dozens of books. She has lectured on every continent. She has even given advice to the president. Today, she's the head of the University of California at San Diego. "It's just a different way of being able to influence the future."

Sputnik I was the first artificial satellite. It was launched by Russia in 1957.

Balls have provided fun for centuries. Early balls were made from stitched up cloth, animal skulls, and pig and cow bladders! Now balls are products of chemistry. In this experiment, you will combine three compounds to create a bouncy ball. The process of creating this ball is called a chemical reaction.

Materials

- borax
- white glue
- cornstarch
- water
- pen

- 2 small cups
- measuring spoons
- stir stick
- small plastic bags

Procedure

1   Label one cup "Borax Solution." Put two tablespoons of warm water into the cup. Add one-half teaspoon of borax powder. Stir with the craft stick until the borax is completely dissolved in the water.

2   Label the other cup "Ball Mix." Put one tablespoon of glue into this cup.

Make a Ball

3 Add one-half teaspoon of the Borax Solution to the Ball Mix. Do not mix.

4 Add one tablespoon of cornstarch to the Ball Mix. Wait 10–15 seconds before mixing.

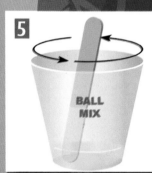

5 Stir the new Ball Mix until it is no longer possible to stir.

6 Take the mixture out of the cup and begin kneading it. Continue until the mixture will hold a ball shape.

7 Store your ball in your baggie to keep it fresh.

Extension Idea

Experiment with the amount of each compound you use. Vary only one compound at a time. Record the amounts of each compound you use and your results.

Glossary

alchemy—early chemistry that did not use the scientific method

atom—the smallest part of an element

CFCs (chlorofluorocarbons)—family of man made chemicals made of chlorine, fluorine, and carbon that damage the ozone layer

chemical bond—a force which binds atoms together to form molecules

chemical reaction—the interaction of two or more molecules producing a chemical change

chemist—a scientist who works in the field of chemistry

chemistry—a branch of science dealing with the structure, composition, and properties of substances

compound—substances made of two or more elements bonded together

crystallography—a branch of science studying the formation and properties of crystals

element—any substance that cannot be broken down into a simpler one by a chemical reaction

freethinker—someone who thinks about new ideas

guillotine—a machine for executing people by beheading them

Law of Conservation of Mass—law that states that matter is neither created nor destroyed in a chemical reaction

mass—the amount of matter an object contains

matter—everything around us

molecule—a group of two or more atoms bonded together

oxygen—an element, usually in gaseous form

ozone layer—the layer of the upper atmosphere that absorbs harmful ultraviolet light

Periodic Table—a table of the chemical elements arranged according to their atomic numbers

physics—science that studies matter, energy, force, and motion

scientific method—way to study a question in science by formulating a question, collecting data about it through observation and experiment, and testing a hypothetical answer

X-ray diffraction—a method that uses the breaking up of X-rays to study the structure of matter

Index

Sally Ride
Science

Sally Ride Science™ is an innovative content company dedicated to fueling young people's interests in science. Our publications and programs provide opportunities for students and teachers to explore the captivating world of science—from astrobiology to zoology. We bring science to life and show young people that science is creative, collaborative, fascinating, and fun.

Image Credits